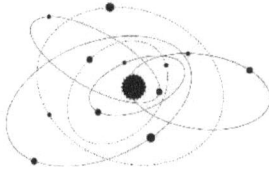

STARSONG

A ZODIAC INSPIRED POETRY COLLECTION

BY KRISTY NICOLLE

First published by Kristy Nicolle, United Kingdom, December 2022

(1st EDITION)
Published December 2022 by Kristy Nicolle
Copyright © 2022 Kristy Nicolle
Edited By- Jaimie Cordall

Poetry Collection

Disclaimer:
This e-book is written in U.K English by personal preference of the author. This is a work of fiction. Names, characters, businesses, places, events and incidents are either the products of the author's imagination or used in a fictitious manner. Any resemblance to actual persons, living or dead, or events is purely coincidental.

ISBN: 978-1-911395-26-3

www.kristynicolle.com

CONTENTS

For those who look at the stars and feel small...

<u>OTHER POETRY COLLECTIONS BY KRISTY NICOLLE</u>

I AM ARCANA- A TAROT INSPIRED POETRY COLLECTION

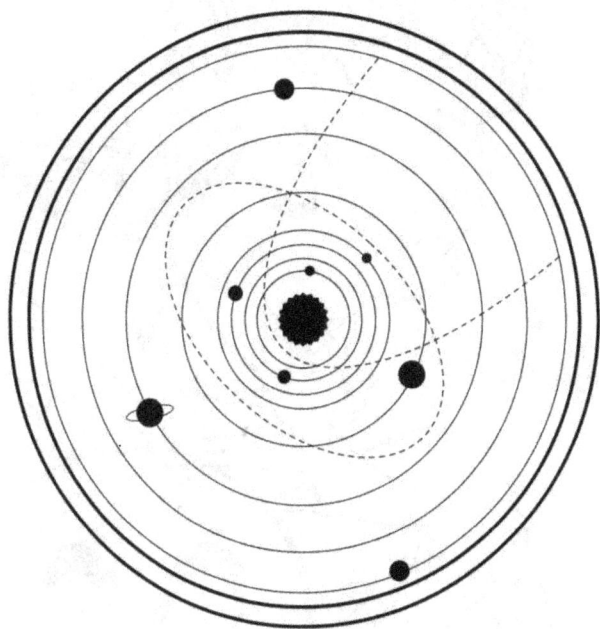

Aries

ARIES

Dates: March 21st-April 20th

Positives: Pioneering, Courageous, Assertive, Competitive, Leaders.

Negatives: Domineering, Selfish, Arrogant, Violent, Impulsive, Intolerant

Element: Fire

Planet: Mars

Symbol: Ram

ORIGIN: Aries is based on a golden ram of Greek mythology. Legend states that Aries, identified with a golden ram, rescued Phrixus and took him to Colchis, where he sacrificed the ram to appease the Gods. Later, Phrixus, faced with death, was saved by a golden ram with wings which flew him to safety.

ARIES

DIGNIFIED

A breath of courage inhaled
then held by a thread.

Her head fights to remain,
tilted high,
beneath the weight of both horns,
despite the fear in their eyes.

GUNPOWDER AND GASOLINE

Gunpowder
waits,
in the chambers of your heart.

Gasoline
swells,
roaring in your veins.

Be patient,
incendiary creature.

All it takes is one divine spark,
for you to go up like a rocket,
lighting up all our tomorrows.

BARBED WIRE TOURNIQUET

I tie it off,
heart in my throat,
pain crashing over my consciousness like a heavy
tide.

This barbed wire tourniquet,
brutal,
cutting deeper,
with every breath.

Yet I cannot resent it,
will not loosen its bite.

My pulse caresses its razor-sharp teeth,
my flesh whimpers at its merciless clutch,
my mind racing,
birthing galaxies with laboured breath.

This life,
the lack,
the suffering,
the endless looming finality of our last approaching
breath.

It is the greatest drug,
the most effective motivation,
to pull from me what might instead stay buried,
beneath the comfortable mundane,
beneath the fog of pleasures and sloth.

This twisted metal vice,
my saviour then.

That which has me searching for inspired action,
otherwise lost to dreams.

That which allows me to pull magic from my veins.

BECOMING POETRY

They warned you about girls like her.
Who shoot from the hip,
take their whiskey neat,
and leave their beds unmade.

Always equipped with a plan,
but never whimsy,
she knows someone,
or is someone,
to get the job done.

Wielding her nature as a blade,
her merciless hurricane will dissect you
with all the ease of butter,
seeking the tools among your entrails,
her answer between your bones.

She is a doer.
With no time for poetry.
And yet, somehow, she has become just that.

ALL OR NOTHING

Licking her bottom lip,
she narrows those eyes,
setting her sights on the impossible.

Her brow creases,
intensity embodied in her smile's lunar crescent,
illuminated beneath the lashes of her ambition's
latest dawn.

Clenching her fists,
she rises from her knees,
grit just beneath the surface of her skin,
iron fizzing restless in her blood.

In the silence, her soul whispers only one truth.

Give me glory or give me death.

Taurus

TAURUS

Dates: April 21st- May 20th

Positives: Tenacious, Punctual, Persistent, Ambitious, Organised, Resourceful

Negatives: Stubborn, Uncompromising, Possessive, Fearful, Rigid, Opinionated.

Element: Earth

Planet: Venus

Symbol: Bull

ORIGIN: Taurus comes from the story of Europa. She was the daughter of King Agenor of Phoenicia and Telephassa. Europa became the object of Zeus' affections, and he appeared to her as a beautiful white bull at the Phoenician waterside. The princess was awestruck by the beauty of the bull and walked over to pet it.

TAURUS

STATUESQUE

Frozen,
fixed in a pose.

Fine as white marble,
balanced stiff on my toes.

I am but art
cultivated by pain,
whittled in love,
long lost and hard gained.

This way, I always will be.
That is just me.

Sameness, a serendipity.

HORNS

Stubborn,
she built the walls of the tower tall,
smooth,
impenetrable,
and unscalable.

Just the way she liked it.

Erected at last,
she dared the world,
to touch her then,
to take her as anything less than an irate bull by
the horns.

WHIMSY TOO LATE

If only I knew then,
what I know now.

To turn back the clock,
and laugh.

To jump in puddles,
with young knees.

To launch from a fraying rope swing,
falling fearlessly into the rapid river of risk,
smiling.

As it is,
I stare at the world now,
with all the whimsy of a child,
through eyes full of cataracts,
skin thin as paper,
and joints adept at betrayal.

What a damn shame.

ROOTS

The idea formed slowly,
a seedling,
pure potential,
germinating in the dark.

But it was the opinion that followed,
spreading wide with strong fingers,
rooting my ways deep,
that sealed my fate,
and banished me from sunlight.

HOME

And through poisonous smog,
scorching, purifying fire,
cleansing, rabid floods,
and seismic, rapturous landslides
still, she stands.

Rooted to the very earth which she embodies so
completely,
she bears her own destruction with arms wide open
to those who call her home.

Gemini

GEMINI

Dates: May 21st- June 20th

Positives: Charming, Adaptable, Perceptive, Quick Witted, Affectionate, Independent.

Negatives: Inconsistent, Manipulative, Opportunistic, Easily Bored, Shallow, Selfish.

Element: Air

Planet: Mercury

Symbol: The Twins

ORIGIN: The constellation of Gemini is made up of two twins, Castor and Pollux. Castor was the mortal son of King Tyndarus, while Pollux was the immortal son of Zeus. Both Castor and Pollux, being identical twins, were inseparable in their looks and actions. Castor was a great horseman, and Pollux was a great fighter.

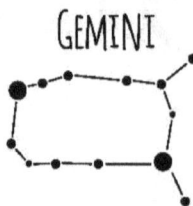

GEMINI

LEAD ME

I take your hand.
A wide-eyed fawn.

You lead me beneath your
endless crisp white sheets.

My bottom lip caught
in the bear trap
between your teeth,
plump and throbbing,
eyes cornered in the cage of your stare.

Vulturine fingers trail
beneath lacy waistbands,
searching
tender silken folds
seeking pleasure as prey.

I open,
surrender,
blooming to life,
letting you in as I exhale,
allowing you to dive deep as I surface.

Take my hand now, desirous lynx.

As I drag you back to this,
the lair of my sweet oblivion.

THORNS

She did not see
thorns embedded in his palm,
dirt smearing his cheek,
nor the blood streaking his elbow.

She was blind to all
but the loveliness
of the sanguine silken roses
held out before her.

THE RIDDLER

From within clouds of promise.

Her voice,
beyond its primal veil,
a siren,
beckons.

Eyes beetle black,
of carapace sheen.

Head of snakes.
Smile of razors.

And yet.

Her words...
those spells
knotted from consonant and vowel,
unravel me at my seams.

I succumb unwillingly,
listening.

Tongue a ladle,
she stirs the dark,
alluring cauldron,
of this,
our most volatile brew.

STEP INTO STARLIGHT

Tread this
the fine razor's edge
of Saturn's outermost ring.

Prick fingertips
upon cold bright stars
let them draw blood.

Bathe nude
in the curious moonlight
exposing every soft angle.

Take my hand
and dive into the sun
just for the hell of it.

THE KNOCK OFF

One of a kind,
she flies.

Painted skin with jagged lines,
she never was one to press rewind.

Steel in her lip,
metal in her stare,
knowing exactly who she is,
existing on a dare.

Proudly,
darkly,
unique.

And yet...
I passed her doppelgänger just yesterday.

Twice.

Cancer

CANCER

Dates: June 22nd to July 22nd

Positives: Nurturing, Sentimental, Caring, Emotional, Protective, Loving, Practical

Negatives: Moody, Insecure, Suspicious, Pessimistic, Clingy

Element: Water

Planet: The Moon

Symbol: The Crab

Origin Story: The constellation of Cancer represents the giant crab that attacked Hercules during the second of the 12 labours he performed as penance for killing his family. The jealous goddess Hera sent it to thwart Hercules as he battled the water serpent Hydra, but he killed it with his club.

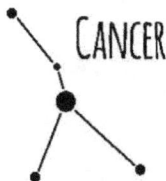

CANCER

MOTHER

Open arms to the masses,
mother's heart,
free for all.

But what about you?
Who is tucking you in at night?

SMALL TALK

Talk to me about bloodshed,
heartache,
late nights and open skies,
fully blooming with stars.

Tell me your life story,
a love story,
some never-ending timeless glory.

Speak of myths and legends,
tales of old,
spirits and magic,
heroes turned bold.

Debate with me our universe.
Your death
My world.
Macbeth!

But please,
whatever you do,
don't talk to me about the weather.

COMING HOME

Tread gentle 'neath the moonlight,
Whorled planks wavering, slight.

Walk back to yourself, child.

Suspended,
above frothing rabid jaws.
Cross this unsteady bridge.

Lean into its creaks and groans,
and find a heart,
with doors,
once more,
flung asunder.

TREADING WATER

I shall dive,
deep,
for buried treasure,
or drown,
gasping,
for precious air.

All I know is I'm done treading water.

FEEL

When they stand before you with tears in their eyes,
and shaking shoulders wracked with sobs,
why is it me,
and only me,
who inevitably asks,
and how does that make you feel?

Leo

LEO

Dates: July 23rd - August 22nd

Positives: Courageous, Determined, Charismatic, Warm-Hearted, Responsible, Loyal

Negatives: Controlling, Demanding, Stubborn, Arrogant, Vain, Quick-Tempered, Boastful.

Element: Fire

Planet: The Sun

Symbol: The Lion

Origin Story: In Greek mythology, Leo is the Nemean Lion, which terrorised the citizens and had a hide that iron, bronze, or stone could not puncture. Killing the lion was one of Hercules' 12 labours, which he had to perform as penance for killing his family.

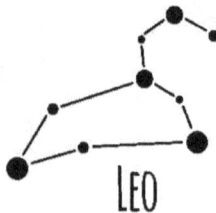

LEO

FAITHFUL

I get down on my knees
at the altar of your love.

Kiss my fingertips,
with red raw lips,
cross my breasts,
with breath held tight.

My eyes flutter shut,
amidst flickering wicks,
gentle as falling in love.

Worrying your scent like a well-loved rosary,
I pray for tomorrow and tomorrow and tomorrow.

LOYALTY

To brand you upon my heart
was to know the pain of
every letter of your name,
but to grin and bear it
screaming love instead.

ROAR

They say
I have a hide
that stone,
nor bronze,
nor iron,
can penetrate.

They say,
I have a heart,
carved,
drily
from ice.

If only they knew,
that I hide the solar flares
of this molten thing,
within my thunder.

Erupting from within my chest,
this vocal,
seismic tremor,
is born from an agony,
too deeply felt,
or a courage,
intrinsic in the heat of my blood.

I know then,

that I am nothing,
if not master,
of my own intense emotional nature.

I know then,
that they know nothing.

That they speak only to hear proof they are bold,
because bearing a roar like mine
would surely shatter their waxen bones,
would surely rise to devour them whole.

SOLAR FLARE

Bow before her,
as planets quiver amid a solar flare.

Scorching embers kiss her feet,
smoke caresses her skin,
tendrils tease her forth,
from this,
a hearth,
stoked by pain and betrayal.

SHIELD

Though she stands centre stage,
shield your eyes,
drop your gaze.

When she drops that robe,
that armour,
this girl's soul won't hesitate to blind you like the sun.

Virgo

VIRGO

Dates: August 23rd- September 22nd

Positives: Analytical, Modest, Responsible, Punctual, Intelligent, Hard-Working, Faithful

Negatives: Perfectionist, Over -Critical, Argumentative, Anxious, Demanding, Self-Righteous

Element: Earth

Planet: Mercury

Symbol: The Virgin

Origin Story: In Greek mythology, Astraea, the daughter of Zeus and Themis, often represents Virgo. As the goddess of Innocence, Virgo was said to have lived amongst us during the Golden Age of man. However, when humanity descended into wickedness and corruption, she fled from Earth for good.

VIRGO

KALEIDOSCOPE

Wicked and superior,
these kaleidoscopes
do turn endlessly
with minds of their own.

Leeching colours,
jagged elegance exposed,
a spinning wheel,
of magnified sentences unserved.

Remove these hazy hazel lenses,
distorted mirrors,
spiderwebbed with cracks,
scorched black by blazes long ash.

Simpler,
truer colours I see
painting all merely mortal,
as only themselves.

REVERENCE

A flower waits for no man to bloom

The punctual then
exist only in reverence.

Not for the flower,
but the fleeting nature of all beauty,
of all life.

THE STORYTELLER

I knew it then,
suddenly,
as surely as I know my mind holds galaxies,
that my heart churns stardust.

Storytelling,
as an act of love.

The raising of a mirror,
a portal to fantasy,
so you might see yourself,
a hero,
a dragon,
a queen,
and no longer feel quite so alone.

PERFUME

Seek me where wisteria climbs,
back to the soil,
face to the sun.

Find me pressed between the earth and the sky,
a flower plucked,
crushed between pages overlooked,
awaiting one, like-minded,
to spread open the story of our roots,
and inhale my perfume.

THE VILLAIN

Halo,
or horns?

Pitchfork,
or sword?

No matter what you choose,
saint or sinner,
you have no control,
who writes you as the villain in their story.

So, make sure you're the hero in your own.

libra

LIBRA

Dates: September 23rd- October 23rd

Positives: Sentimental, Peace-Loving, Easy Going, Reliable, Sincere, Sweet, Logical

Negatives: Impatient, Indecisive, Co-dependent, Gullible, Self-Indulgent, Sulky, Complainer

Element: Air

Planet: Venus

Symbol: The Scales of Justice

Origin Story: According to Greek mythology, Libra is related to the Greek Goddess of Justice, Themis, whose daughter, Astraea, went up to heaven and became the constellation of Virgo. Both goddesses carried the scales of justice, which became the symbol for Libra.

LIBRA

CHOOSING PEACE

How painful it is,
to live in a world,
free-falling through time,
clinging to every moment,
with no clue,
no inkling,
which could be your very last.

How dizzying,
to stand in a world,
spinning at the speed of sound,
to know,
you know nothing,
and cannot touch the stars.

I wonder,
falling,
spinning,
if perhaps then,
they did not make me for stillness,
but velocity instead.

I let go,
and suddenly,
at that same speed,
that rush,
that din,
that passing moment,
all is quiet,

as though I had been at peace all along
and had only to allow it.

THE STALLING HEART

The heart stalls.
Over
and over again.

Too many revs.
Losing that bite point.
Grinding its gears.

Why let it drive?
I hear you ask,
impatient.

Well,
I sigh,
lovelorn.

It is the only one
who knows the way to paradise.

DISTILL

These words
they bleed
from fingertips.

All curves,
slashes,
and sudden stops.

Though my soul spills,
spirited calligraphy,
these swirls are not their home.

They, I might bleed
but they are not me.

Never me,
in words alone.

HALFWAY

Meet me halfway,
somewhere amid the dawn and dusk of our days,
you will step forward with arms wide open
and find me waiting.

A half-drunk bottle of vintage wine,
a book spine long cracked,
yellowed pages splayed mid-way,
tea steeping cold on the stove,
curtains neither drawn nor gaping.

I am sitting on the floor,
floating betwixt passing moments,
a real girl swept in an unfinished world,
waiting for you to write my ending.

Meet me halfway,
and balance this chaos,
so it turns beautiful,

WHO AM I?

The question of who I am lies wholly unanswerable.
A lexicon of infinite unknowability.
A riddle of timeless complexity, of intricate
dissonance.

Why, in a universe of endless possibilities,
of far-reaching facets,
and options aplenty,
would I cage myself within boxes of nouns of
syllables too quickly spoken?

Put simply...

Why be a star,
when you can be the whole damn universe?

Scorpio

SCORPIO

Date: October 23 - November 21

Positive Traits: Focused, Intense, Purposeful, Charismatic, Cunning, Competitive, Intuitive, Powerful, Mysterious.

Negative Traits: Aggressive, Obstinate, Intolerant, Possessive, Manipulative, Destructive, Jealous, Resentful.

Element: Water

Planet: Pluto

Symbol: The Scorpion

Origin: Scorpio, in Greek Mythology, comes from the story of Orion. He and Artemis were hunting partners. Orion was a great hunter who had boasted that he could kill any animal on Earth. Gaia (Earth) was angry with Orion and sent Scorpius, a giant scorpion, to kill him. The two fought and both were killed in the struggle. From their ashes rose the constellations Scorpius and Orion.

SCORPIO

VENOM

That whip-lashing tongue,
sharp as jagged glass
and thrice as fragile.

It launches a venom
brewed of my smallness
made potent in the heat of terror
a compound catalysed by gritty, irritant anxiety.

Poison sparks from my tongue
into their faces
and yet it is I who crumples.

It is only me
who weeps.

SHADES OF RED

Sanguine yet unsated
blood trickles from her fingers.

Crimson misery pools at her feet,
reflecting fury,
absolution,
destruction.
Born in love.

His body,
cold and clotted,
like the sour milk
his mother fed him

Her blade,
the double-edged sword
embedded deep in the stone
of his heart.

Pulling it asunder,
holy in her viciousness.
It sprays her face
vermillion.

A verisimilitude of
his long-assumed humanity.

She is a Queen,
long foretold.

A creature of passion,
and undeniable craving
to gain orbit
in a foreign universe.

Her wrath crowns her
with the shimmering
ruby glory
of her uncompromising mission.

To fulfil her destiny.

To become another's
unequivocal,
undeniable,
world.

AN HONEST DISSECTION

They feared her.

Plain and simple.

Her words a scorpion's sting.
Cutting right to the heart,
no anaesthesia,
severing every string
with a scalpel of unspoken truths.

MONSTROSITY

How sad I am to discover
the Scorpion's immortality
ensured not by his gleaming carapace,
nor the ingenious evolution of its
ancient and long surviving design,
but by our own violence.

A mighty creature
of intricate,
beautiful viciousness,
made stars only
because first
we made it a villain.

It is,
undoubtedly,
I see,
one of the universe's
most ingenious arachnids.

Walking the earth for three hundred million years,
dancing in the face of love,
glowing beneath the velvet night.

What a shame then,
this most holy of minute Gods
only ascended the heavens,
because first,

we made it a weapon.

X-RAY

And like an X-Ray
I saw your lies
in but a moment,
a glorious monochrome symphony.

Darling,
You should know by now,
no lead thick enough,
no deceit so beautiful,
exists to shield you from me,
or from yourself.

Sagittarius

SAGITTARIUS

Dates: *23rd November- 21st December*

Positive Traits: *Optimistic, Freedom Loving, Jovial, Good Humoured, Honest, Straight Forward, Intellectual, Philosophical, Faithful*

Negatives Traits: *Blindly Optimistic, Careless, irresponsible, superficial, tactless, restless.*

Element: *Fire*

Planet: *Jupiter*

Symbol: *The Archer*

Origin: *Greek mythology associates Sagittarius with the centaur Chiron, who mentored Achilles, a Greek hero of the Trojan War, in archery. Sagittarius, the half human, and half horse is the centaur of mythology, the learned healer whose higher intelligence forms a bridge between Earth and Heaven.*

SAGITTARIUS

HOOFBEATS

Hoofbeats.

Clattering,
within my ears,
Pulsing,
treading restless blood.

Hoofbeats.

Pounding,
kicking my heart,
Slamming,
thunder against my ribcage.

Hoofbeats.

Galloping,
devouring the land of my soul.
Climbing,
craggy fatal peaks of curiosity,

I stand,
hair whipped back,
hearing them still.

At last.

Silence.

I inhale the air
of this unknown place,
of this new world
just for me.

Fences kicked down,
lie, splintered, asunder,
felled by those same hooves,
that punish my shrinking
with cruel, joyous bucking.

Wildness that will not be tamed,
satiated only by the next sunset,
river around the bend,
endless sprawl of the untread path.

So, I succumb.

Allow it to run,
into the sun,
beyond the horizon,
trampling fences erected
long before I was born.

CUPID'S BOW

That bow,
small crease,
upon your lip.

Twisted,
pulled wide,
over tear-inducing pearls.

You notched your intent,
with twinkling eyes,
sighted truth
with small, measured sighs.

It was not
The accuracy
Of that smile,
Shot straight to the heart.

But the target
sought through mere glass,
where others met only scars.

You could not have missed,
If even you tried,
For you saw past my walls,
my wounds,
and my pride.

SIMPLE WORDS

You need no arrowhead,
of silver or gold,
nor cast in steel,
from an iron-age mould.

Your words are piercing enough.

OPPORTUNIST

And when all they saw
was a girl obsessed
with black ink
on white paper,
you saw a mind
turned technicolour.

THE BRIDGE

A golden connection
woven between
my prefrontal cortex
and the land of dreams.

An idea glistening,
hung by a thread,
inspiration aplenty,
followed by dread.

Am I worthy,
of a bridge
so Godly made?
In the darkness
of night
where the muses do aid?

Can I do it?
Can I learn?
Spin galaxies into stories?
Capture suns' deadly burn?

I know not why I'm chosen
Or why this path's open
But I know I must walk it
With words seeming mere token.

A storyteller it's made me,
from now until never,

love it or hate it,
this tether's forever.

Capricorn

CAPRICORN

Dates: December 22nd - January 19

Positives: Practical, Traditional, Loyal, Ambitious, Responsible, Hard-Working, Organized.

Negatives: Pessimistic, Stubborn, Blunt, Unforgiving, Rigid, Condescending, Moody.

Element: Earth

Planet: Saturn

Symbol: Sea Goat

Origin: Capricornus gets its name from a Greek myth in which the god Pan was transformed into a half-goat, half-fish when he dived into the Nile River to escape the giant Typhon.

CAPRICORN

TIMELESS DANCE

Living,
with one foot in tomorrow's sunrise,
and the other
mired in today's noontime glow,
I tread only time.

Life,
a stage for perfection,
awaits only the next great leap,
that might bring
the crowd to its feet.

Purposefully,
I pirouette on
through mundane routine.

Every step
is a new work of art.
Every breath
choreographed by hope
that one day
the final Grand Jete
might come.

These small,
prepared,
discrete steps,
are essence itself,
are all.

74

One day,
this subtle toe turn,
the minutely tuned angle of my neck,
will propel me skyward,
to be suspended forever
in triumph

HIDDEN FIRE

Fragile,
It appears.

A glass ornament on a mantlepiece.

Forget then that glass comes from
scorching heat,
blistering fever,
and searing intensity,
at your peril.

KNEES

Driven to,
she is sturdier now
than ever before.

Coiled above,
she is ready,
sprung and waiting.

Resting upon,
she is finding strength,
to resurrect exquisitely.

Never underestimate
the power
of falling to your knees.

It is where the universe hears your pain and your
plea.

It is where you find the strength again to stand.

DARK BRILLIANCE

She was not the brightest star in the sky,
but his devouring darkness turned her brilliant.

PROCRASTINATION NATION

Their Queen above all.

A vision of the world as it should be
held tightly in the palms of her hands.

She knew,
the solution was simple,
it was...

Aquarius

AQUARIUS

Dates: January 20th - February 18th

Positive Traits: Friendly, Creative, Idealistic, Humanitarian, Original, Individualistic, Independent.

Negative Traits: Detached, Runs from reality, Chaotic, Contradictory, Radical, Unpredictable, Self-Conscious

Element: Air

Planet: Uranus

Symbol: Water-Bearer

Origin: One of the oldest constellations in the sky, Greek Mythology tells us that Aquarius was Ganymede, a young boy kidnapped by Zeus. Zeus sent his pet Eagle, Aquila, to steal Ganymede from the fields where he was watching over sheep. Later, Ganymede became the cupbearer for the gods, hence why the symbol of Aquarius. Look closely at the constellation itself and you may see the form of a young boy dangling in the sky overhead.

AQUARIUS

DREAMWALKING

If I could run
across this dark cement,
over trash and cigarette ash,
and burst through clouds instead...

Trust me,
I would.

BEARER

Torn between the river and the field,
vase cupped in both hands,
he pours generously,
with no motivation but love.

Neither earth,
nor water,
but air,
mysterious and free,
a subtle nudge to nurse the spark.

He stands,
wholly himself,
giving from abundance alone,
letting life find a way,
and inspiration seek its own path to fruition.

Maybe not today,
maybe not tomorrow,
but soon,
in this very spot,
precious creation will bloom again,
his real gift that of no expectation.

BOUND

Twined from dreams and starlight seen,
this long-bound bird cuts loose routine.

WONDERLAND

Ah Alice,
I envy your tumble.

Yet, no wonderland do I require.

I hunger only for
the darkness of soil,
and twisting warrens
away from the world.

HEAL

There is no magic potion.
No serum or lotion.

No miracle cure.
Of that, I am sure.

There is only breath

Your ability to take the next.
And the next.
And the next.

Pisces

PISCES

Dates: February 19th- March 20th

Positive Traits: Selfless, Kind, Romantic, Forgiving, Creative, Intuitive, Artistic

Negative Traits: Overly Sensitive, Melancholy, Pessimistic, Procrastinator, Temperamental

Element: Water

Planet: Neptune

Symbol: Fish

Origin: Much like Capricorn, this story also features two gods trying to escape the monster Typhon. In the myth of Pisces, Aphrodite and Eros both jumped into the river during their escape from the giant, turned into fish, and swam away.

PISCES

RIVER CHILD

Ripples of dissent
I've found,
wading against the current
struggling to stand.

Sediment disturbed,
my memories churn,
cast now in rapid froth
threatening to drown.

The sky weeps
as do I,
enshrouded by behemoth hungry banks,
and grey light,
weighed down by urban woes.

Stone shards
let blood,
surface tension shatters,
and a child long since lost
decisively draws gasping breath.

Face turned toward the sun.
the forest breathes her in,
and I remember.

Exhaling adult tensity,
the dreamer smiles,
re-born at last.

STITCHES

An open wound
I could not suffer,
I cauterised it all.

Burning memory
of your touch away,
stemming the flow of
rose-tinted memories,
stitching together the story
of how it all went wrong,
I left only raw flesh
and jagged scars behind.

SLICE

So desperate to feel,
I slice
with nails,
with blade,
with tongue.

This world,
not enough.

I draw blood,
willing emptiness at last.

ANCHOR

Let me lean into your steel, my love.

Tie me fast upon the shore.

So I might drift away,
upon the waves,
and dream a little more.

VEIN OF GOLD

My emotion runs deep,
a thick vein of gold.

I am done waiting
for whomever might
mine me from obscurity.

Instead,
I will swing the blade,
shattering stone,
grinding doubt.

I shall bathe in the sunlight
by my own hand,
and shine.

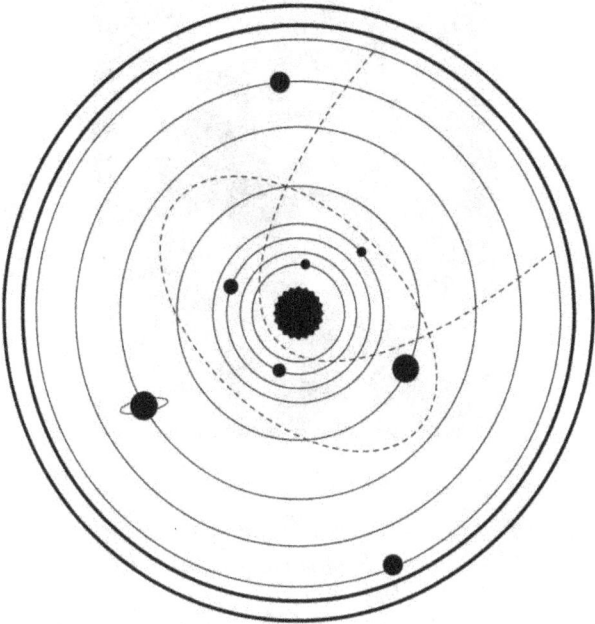

ABOUT THE AUTHOR

29-year-old British writer Kristy Nicolle is achieving freedom from the pain of her Ehlers Danlos Syndrome diagnosis by bringing fantasy worlds to life for her readers. Kristy enjoys spending time in her fuzzy PJs with her kitty arch nemesis, Moo, and loves all things mermaids, unicorns, and glitter!

Award-winning author of over a million published words, Kristy Nicolle is currently working on a supersized series called The Kristy Nicolle Fantasy Infiniverse.

StarSong is Kristy Nicolle's second poetry collection.

Keep up to date with Kristy Nicolle @ www.kristynicolle.com

Fantasy Romance Titles by Kristy Nicolle

The Queens of Fantasy Saga

Trilogy One- The Tidal Kiss Trilogy

(Mermaids)

The Kiss That Killed Me

The Kiss That Saved Me

The Kiss That Changed me

Tidal Kiss Short Stories

Waiting For Gideon

Beyond The Shallows

Tidal Kiss Novellas

Vexed

Trilogy Two- The Ashen Touch Trilogy

(Demons and The Underworld)

The Opal Blade

The Onyx Hourglass

The Obsidian Shard

Ashen Touch Short Stories

A Touch of Smoke And Snow

Trilogy Three- The Aetherial Embrace Trilogy

(Angels, Fae, Dragons, Unicorns)

Indigo Dusk

Violet Dawn

Lavender Storm

Higher Plains Short Stories

Ambrosia Nights

Queens of Fantasy Saga Book 10- Title TBA

DYSTOPIAN ROMANCE TITLES BY KRISTY NICOLLE

(Arranged Blind Marriage By Science)
Something Blue- A Standalone Dystopian Romance Novel

ACKNOWLEDGEMENTS

I want to thank all the readers who have been so incredibly supportive throughout my poetry journey, without you all I never would have known I had a knack for poetry, or that my poetry was worth publishing. As ever my undying gratitude goes to my wonderful family, Jaimie Cordall, Winters Rage, Jenna Martinez, Leanna Rae Herr, and all the other Infiniverse Explorers who have helped make this collection a reality!

Stay magical!
Kristy Nicolle x

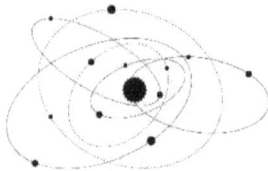

www.ingramcontent.com/pod-product-compliance
Lightning Source LLC
Chambersburg PA
CBHW031628040426
42452CB00007B/730